D0570062

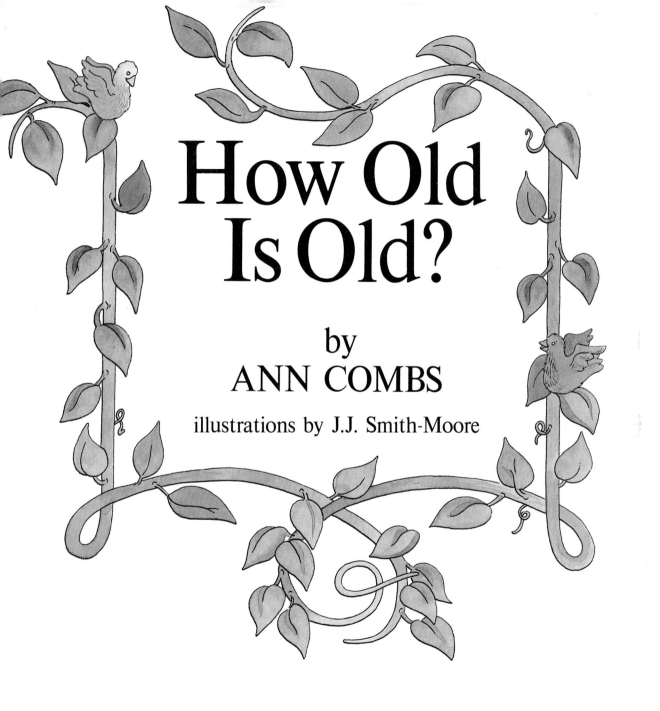

How Old Is Old?

by
ANN COMBS

illustrations by J.J. Smith-Moore

Library of Congress Cataloging-in-Publication Data
Combs, Ann, 1935–
How old is old?/by Ann Combs.
p. cm.
Summary: With examples from nature, including chickadees,
trees, stars, and snakes, Alistair's grandfather explains to him
that being old is a relative concept.
ISBN 0-8431-2219-6: $8.95
[1. Old age—Fiction. 2. Grandfathers—Fiction.
3. Nature—Fiction. 4. Stories in rhyme.] I. Title.
PZ8.3.C687 1988   87-25843
[E]—dc19   CIP
AC

Published by Price Stern Sloan, Inc.
360 North La Cienega Boulevard, Los Angeles, California 90048

ISBN: 0-8431-2219-6

To Sara

There once was a boy, Alistair was his name,
Whose grandfather's birthday and his were the same.
Since they both had been born on the thirteenth of May,
Well, not the same year, but at least the same day.
Each time one said, "Happy Birthday to you,"
The other replied "And the same to you too."

Then one year, I think Alistair had turned four,
And his grandad was fifty or sixty or more,
The young boy climbed up in his grandfather's chair,
And they rocked for awhile, just the two of them there.
And then all of a sudden, or so I've been told,
Young Alistair asked, "Is it true that you're old?"

"What makes you say that?" his grandfather replied
As he smiled at the boy sitting there by his side.
"Do <u>you</u> think that I'm old? Do I seem old to you?"
And Alistair said, as he stared at his shoe,
"I really don't know. I just thought you must be,
"Since you're older than Mommy and Daddy and me."

"Well no, I'm not old, though my hair's turning white
"And I can't see to read if there's not enough light,
"And I can't go upstairs without puffing or sweating
"And things I've remembered I now keep forgetting,
"But no, I'm not old, though I may wheeze and snore,
"I don't plan to be old for a lot of years more."

"Well how old is old then? That's what I want to know.
"Is it ninety? A hundred? A million or so?
"Mommy says that our dog's getting old and he's ten.
"So please can you tell me? Can you tell me when,
"Do things get to be old? 'Cause I don't understand."
"Oh all right, I will try, Alistair," said the man.

And as he leaned back and while scratching his head,
He thought for awhile and then here's what he said.

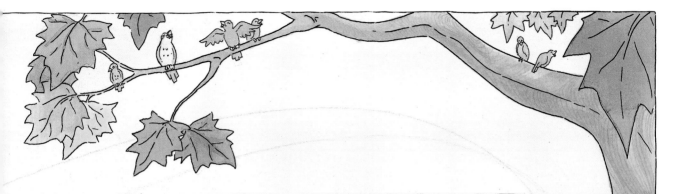

"The chickadees one sees in trees,
"Playing in the morning breeze,
"Never wheeze, rarely sneeze,
"Don't get twinges in their knees,
"Till they reach eight, or nine, and then,
"A chickadee is old at ten."
But . . .

"The elephant with lengthy nose
"And floppy ears and calloused toes,
"Whose tusks must take a week to brush,
"And who gets grumpy if she's rushed
"Looks old and wrinkled from her youth.
"But if you want to know the truth,
"That elephant, so slow and weighty,
"Feels fairly spry up till she's eighty."
On the other hand . . .

"Spiders spin the webs they're in,
"In meadows, barns and trees.
"On windy days they sail away,
"Just floating on the breeze.
"They dine on flies, I don't know why,
"It's something I would shun.
"They often scurry, and perhaps they hurry,
"Because they're old at one."
And . . .

"Though they're old at one, the sun and the stars
"And our own planet, Earth, and Venus and Mars
"Have been spinning around for billions of years,
"Which seems old to me, and yet it appears
"That they plan to keep spinning and spinning. And so
"Perhaps they're still young. I really don't know."
But . . .

"They say it's true, the kangaroo
"Lives in a pocket when he's new.
"And then by four, I've heard before,
"He's leaping twenty feet or more.
"He's also keen on being mean,
"When he turns old around nineteen."
And . . .

"Did you know there are trees 'bout as tall as my knees?
"And they're planted in dishes, I'm told.
"People call them bonsai, and they may not grow high,
"But some are six hundred years old.

"Then again, if you please, there are also some trees
"That are so tall they're touching the sky.
"They're a sight to behold, and two thousand years old.
"No wonder they've grown up so high."
But . . .

"A bee is young in springtime,
"And while the birds are singing,
"She flits among the daffodils
"And saves some time for stinging.
"A bee's still strong in summer,
"Still buzzing left and right,

"She barely stops to catch her breath
"From early dawn till night.
"But then in mid-September,
"She slows down to a crawl,
"And maybe feels a little stiff,
"Because she's old in fall."

"And have you heard the mayfly,
"That's always born in May,
"Is old in just an hour or two
"And only lives one day?"
While . . .

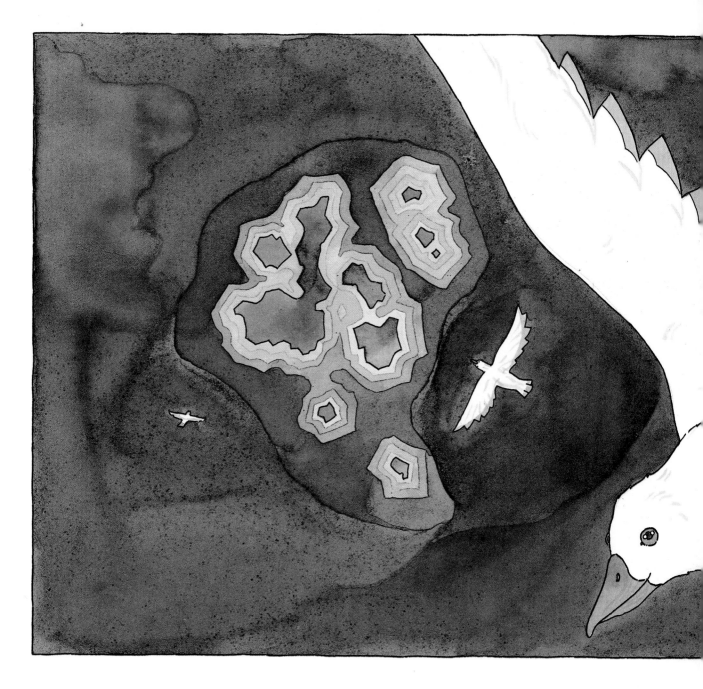

"In faraway Galapagos,
"Just off the coast of Ecuador,
"Are lots of giant tortoises
"That live a hundred years or more.
"And though they might look old to us
"When they're just fifty-five or so,
"Since all their skin is leathery,

"And all their lumbering steps are slow.
"They're not, you see, because the years
"They've left to live are plenty,
"And they are only middle-aged
"When they're a hundred-twenty."
Finally . . .

"A boa that's young and scaly and green
"Can glide through the jungle and never be seen.
"He can zip up a tree. He can slide down a vine.
"He can give you a hug that'll splinter your spine.
"But when he turns eighteen or nineteen or more,
"And slipping's not easy and sliding's a chore,
"And all twenty feet of him are usually sore,
"He knows he is old then. Can you understand?
"A boa is old when *you're* hardly a man."

And Alistair, just lately three,
Still sitting on his grandad's knee,
Said, "Yes, I think so. Yes, I see,
"You're young for a star, I'm old for a bee."

Lyon has been a Pagan parent since March 1994, when her daughter was born. She has followed a Pagan path all her adult life. That is over 25 years give or take a few years. She began to actively call herself Pagan in 1985 after she read "Drawing Down the Moon" by Margot Adler. She continually reads and researchs to achieve a better understanding of the Pagan Path and deepen her spiritual connection to the Goddess and God.

Lyon is an eclectic Pagan living in Eastern Missouri. She has written articles for Pagan publications both on-line and in print including PagaNet News (now renamed IF...), The Seeker Journal, NewWitch, Crescent Magazine, Elements Magazine, The Witch's Voice and The Pagan-Wiccan Times.

She has been a working artist since 1981, when she received an Associate of Applied Science degree from the Fashion Institute of Technology. She continued her training at the School of Visual Arts where she received a Bachelor of Fine Arts in 1988. She has exhibited her watercolor paintings in art shows internationally. Her fine art paintings grace both public and private collections. Her illustration work has been featured in assorted publications, from books and magazines to corporate collateral materials and advertisements.

You can visit Lyon on her website www.magicalchild.handcraftedpagan.com. She lives with her husband, her daughter and two crotchety cats of undetermined ancestry.

MAGICAL BOOKS FOR MAGICAL KIDS
Stories from Magical Child Books

An Ordinary Girl, A Magical Child
Take a joyful romp with Rabbit around the wheel of the Year as she learns about herself and her Pagan Ways in the first fully illustrated Pagan children's book to explore Wiccan magic, customs and holidays through a child's point of view.
ISBN-13 978-0-9796834-3-5
$16.95 Hardcover

Aidan's First Full Moon Circle
An enchanting, fictional tale of a Wiccan nighttime gathering will engage young readers with magical images while introducing some coven ritual basics.
ISBN-13 978-0-9796834-4-2
$16.95 Hardcover

Watchers
Coming May 2008

Watchers
Who's hiding in corners and watching in the dark? A trap is set and our hero receives a big surprise when the watchers are finally captured. Young readers will request this bouncy bedtime tale even after they know the mystery.
ISBN-13 978-0-9796834-5-9
$16.95 Hardcover

Buy them at your local book store or use this convenient coupon for ordering.
Shades of White • 301 Tenth Avenue • Crystal City, MO 63019

Please send me the Magical Child Books I have checked, for which I am enclosing $ _____ (Please add $5.00 to cover postage and handling) Send Check or Money Order (no cash or C.O.D.s) or charge by MasterCard or Visa. Prices and numbers are subject to change without notice.
_____ An Ordinary Girl, A Magical Child   _____ Aidan's First Full Moon Circle   _____ Watchers

Name: _____

Card#: _____   Exp Date: _____   Phone: _____

Address: _____

City: _____   State: _____   Zip: _____

For faster ordering by credit card call **314-740-0361** or visit us online at **www.paganchildrensbookpublishing.info**

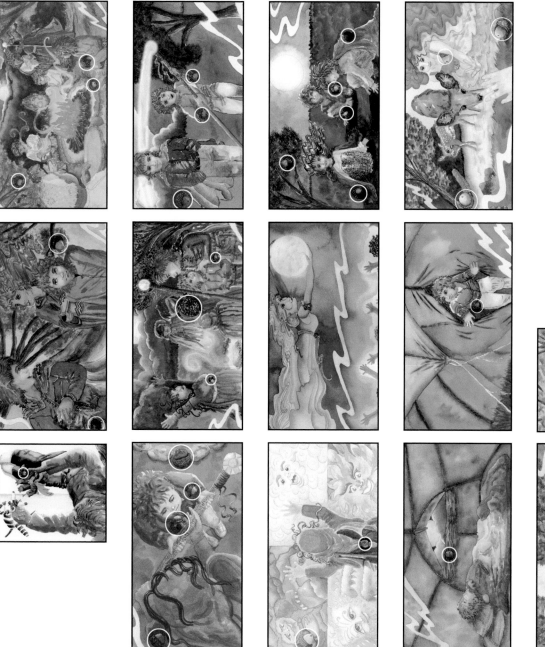

Glossary of Terms

(as used in this book - visit www.handcraftedpagan.com for teaching guides)

Circle – A border between the everyday world (outside) and the enchanted world (within), where magic can happen more easily.

Cast Circle – The beginning of a Wiccan ritual to form a holy space. Wiccans believe the Circle holds in the energy from the ritual and keeps out energy from other places.

Coven – A group of witches (or Wiccans) meeting regularly, working together to make magic, share stories, and learn about Wicca.

Earth Power – Special places on Earth called ley lines, have extra natural energy. In this tale, Earth Power is a make-believe place on one of them.

Elements – Earth in the North, Air in the East, Fire in the South and Water in the West. These are special parts of Nature which help make the Circle and the people inside it strong.

Harvest Moon – Full moons each have a name. The Harvest Moon is the full moon closest to September 21.

High Priestess – The female leader of a coven, and organizer of the ritual.

Release – During a ritual, Wiccans create and gather as much energy as they can. When they have collected a lot, they send it to a plan, place or person chosen before the ritual.

They cleaned up and prepared to leave. Mama glanced over her shoulder at Aidan. "Did you have a good time?"

Aidan nodded. He relished meeting the deer and fawn.

He couldn't wait until the next Full Moon.

He opened his eyes The deer and fawn were gone. Aidan hugged himself. His body tingled with energy.

"Wow, I met Goddess."

Aidan smelled pancakes. His stomach growled. He sprinted to the campsite.